Lives and Times

MOTHER TERESA

John Barraclough

Heinemann
LIBRARY

www.heinemann.co.uk
Visit our website to find out more information about Heinemann Library books.

To order:
 Phone 44 (0) 1865 888066
 Send a fax to 44 (0) 1865 314091
Visit the Heinemann Bookshop at www.heinemann.co.uk to browse our catalogue and order online.

First published in Great Britain by Heinemann Library,
Halley Court, Jordan Hill, Oxford OX2 8EJ,
a division of Reed Educational and Professional Publishing Ltd.
Heinemann is a registered trademark of Reed Educational and Professional Publishing Ltd.

OXFORD MELBOURNE AUCKLAND
JOHANNESBURG BLANTYRE GABORONE
IBADAN PORTSMOUTH (NH) USA CHICAGO

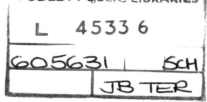
Designed by Ken Vail Graphic Design, Cambridge
Illustrated by Barbra Lofthouse
Originated by Dot Gradations
Printed by South China Printing in Hong Kong/China

ISBN 0 431 13441 3 (hardback)
05 04 03 02 01
10 9 8 7 6 5 4 3 2 1

ISBN 0 431 13446 4 (paperback)
05 04 03 02 01
10 9 8 7 6 5 4 3 2 1

British Library Cataloguing in Publication Data

Barraclough, John
  Mother Teresa. – (Lives and times) (Take-off!)
  1.Teresa, Mother, 1910– – Juvenile literature
  2.Women missionaries – India – Biography – Juvenile literature
  3.Missionaries – India – Biography – Juvenile literature
  4.Nuns – India – Biography – Juvenile literature
  I.Title
  266.2'092

Acknowledgements

The publishers would like to thank the following for permission to reproduce photographs: Andes Press Agency / Carlos Reyes – Manzo, p. 19; Camera Press Ltd / S.K. Dutt, pp. 17, 18, 22

Cover photograph reproduced with permission of Frank Spooner.

Our thanks to Sue Graves and Hilda Reed for their advice and expertise in the preparation of this book.

Every effort has been made to contact copyright holders of any material reproduced in this book. Any omissions will be rectified in subsequent printings if notice is given to the publishers.

Contents

Any words appearing in the text in bold, **like this**, are explained in the Glossary.

Early life

Mother Teresa was born in 1910 in Albania. At that time she was called Agnes **Bejaxhiu**. When she was a little girl, Agnes talked to many **missionaries**. She wanted to help people.

missionaries

Agnes listening to missionaries.

Agnes was not an only child. She had a brother and a sister.

Sister Teresa

Sister Teresa teaching at a girls' school in India.

pupils

When she was 18, Agnes became a **nun**. She was called Sister Teresa. She went to India to teach. She loved her work, but it upset her that so many people lived in **slums**.

Sister Teresa taught at St Mary's High School convent in Calcutta.

5

First clinic and school

Teresa felt that God wanted her to help. She left the girls' school where she was working. She started a very simple **clinic** where she could help sick people from the **slums**.

Sick people from the slums coming to Teresa's clinic for help.

Teresa

When Teresa started up the clinic, she started wearing Indian clothes.

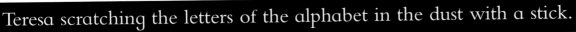
Teresa scratching the letters of the alphabet in the dust with a stick.

letters of the
Indian alphabet

The children who lived in the slums had no
schools to go to. Teresa started to teach them
in the street. She scratched the letters of the
alphabet in the dust with a stick.

Mother Teresa's nuns

Two years later, Teresa asked some other **nuns** to work with her. Her name became Mother Teresa.

All the nuns wearing long blue and white Indian robes like Mother Teresa.

blue and white robes

Mother Teresa taking the dying woman to hospital.

One day, Mother Teresa found a homeless woman dying in the street. She begged the hospital to let the woman in. Otherwise the woman would have died out in the street.

Mother Teresa and the nuns who worked with her were known as the **Missionaries** of Charity.

A home for the dying

Mother Teresa knew that she had to do something to help the poor people who had no one to care for them when they were sick. She said that nobody should have to die in the street.

In 1952, Mother Teresa opened a home for the **destitute** and dying. The home was called **Kalighat**. Anyone was welcome here, and everyone was cared for.

The nuns caring for people at Kalighat.

Children

Mother Teresa always cared deeply for everyone. She looked after many children whose parents could not look after them.

Mother Teresa looking after a child.

nun

The Shishu Bavan children's home.

She and her **nuns** opened a children's home called **Shishu Bavan**. All children can go there and be cared for. No matter how full it is, the nuns say, 'There is always room for one more.'

Mother Teresa opened more than 60 schools, orphanages and homes for the dying around the world.

Lepers

Lepers are people who have a serious disease called **leprosy**. Many lepers are thrown out of their homes. Mother Teresa provided a home for lepers in India.

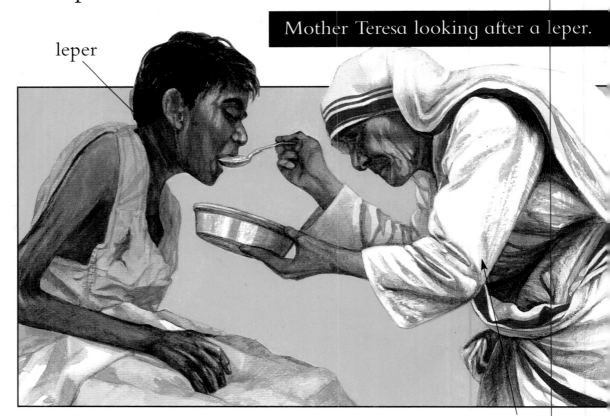

Mother Teresa looking after a leper.

leper

Mother Teresa

One home was called Shanti Nagar which means 'Town of Peace'.

Prizes

Nobel Peace Prize

Mother Teresa being given the Nobel Peace Prize in 1979.

Mother Teresa is famous for her work with homeless children and people who are ill and very poor. In 1979, she got an important prize, called the **Nobel Peace Prize**. This was to thank her for her work. She died in 1997.

Photographs

When Mother Teresa left home to become a **nun** in India, she gave a photograph of herself to her aunt. The photograph shows what she looked like as a young woman.

The photograph Teresa gave to her aunt.

Read page 5 again to find out how old Teresa was when she left home to become a nun.

sick child

Mother Teresa

This photograph is one of many which shows Mother Teresa doing her work.

Mother Teresa worked with poor and ill people in many places. Her name is known everywhere.

Many photographers have visited Mother Teresa's homes. They have taken lots of pictures of her and her **nuns**.

food

This picture shows her nuns giving out food to the poor.

This photograph shows Mother Teresa visiting children in London.

Mother Teresa worked a lot in India. She also worked in about 100 other countries.

Scrapbooks and letters

Mother Teresa's friend, Father Henry, kept a scrapbook. It tells us about Mother Teresa. On 16 August 1948, he wrote that Mother Teresa wanted to work with poor people in **Calcutta**.

This is a page from Father Henry's scrapbook.

Can you read the date at the very top of this page from Father Henry's scrapbook?

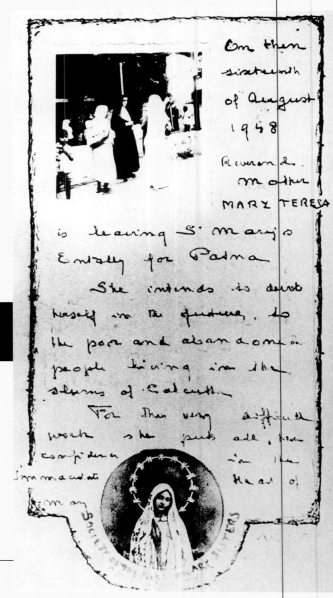

MISSIONARIES OF CHARITY.
54-A, Lower Circular Road,
Calcutta · _____ . 195 .

My dear Mark
Thank you
for your gift.
Love Jesus and
Mary God bless
You & Your Sister
and little Baby
M. Teresa.

Mother Teresa's signature

Mother Teresa wrote this letter to a charity that helps people with leprosy.

Mother Teresa wrote many thank-you letters to people who helped with her work.

Now see if you can read Mother Teresa's letter.

Signs and stamps

Kalighat, the home for people who are very poor and ill or dying, is also called Nirmal Hriday. This means 'the Place of the Pure Heart'. The sign you can see is written in English and Bengali. It is by the entrance to the home.

English

Bengali

The sign is written in English and Bengali.

name of prize

Mother Teresa

नोबेल शान्ति पुरस्कार: माँ टेरेसा
NOBEL PEACE PRIZE 1979:
MOTHER TERESA

PRO·PACE·ET·FRATERNITATE·GENTIUM

30 भारत INDIA
1980

stamp price

country

The Indian post office made this stamp to say thank you to Mother Teresa.

When Mother Teresa got the **Nobel Peace Prize**, the Indian post office made this special stamp.

23

Glossary

Bejaxhiu You say *boh-sha-shoo.*

Calcutta a big city in India. You say *kal-KUH-ta.*

clinic place where you go to see a nurse or doctor

destitute very poor

Kalighat home that Mother Teresa opened. You say *ka-lee-gat.*

leper person who has the disease leprosy. You say *leppa.*

leprosy a skin disease

missionary person who travels to other countries to tell people about his or her religion. You say *mish-yun-erry.*

Nobel Peace Prize prize that is given to people who have done something very special to help other people

nun woman who follows the Christian religion, and who lives as part of a group of nuns. They all follow the same rules. They pray, and often help other people.

Shishu Bhavan You say *shi-shoo ba-van.*

slums places with very poor houses with no running water, electricity or gas. Often they are built from spare wood, plastic and tin sheeting, or whatever people can find.

Index

24

Titles in the *Lives and Times* series include:

Hardback   0 431 13440 5

Hardback   0 431 13442 1

Hardback   0 431 13443 X

Hardback   0 431 13441 3

Find out about the other titles in this series on our website www.heinemann.co.uk/library